Baby Whales Drink Milk

by **Barbara Juster Esbensen**

illustrated by **Lambert Davis**

HOUGHTON MIFFLIN

Boston • Atlanta • Dallas • Geneva, Illinois • Palo Alto • Princeton

Baby Whales Drink Milk

Whales are huge sea animals. They live in the ocean the way fish do. A whale's enormous body is shaped like a fish. But it is not a fish. It is a mammal.

Humans are mammals. Cats, dogs, horses, and pigs are mammals too.

They all feed their babies milk that comes from their bodies.

Whales are mammals. Whale
babies drink milk too.

Whales are very different from fish. Most fish hatch from eggs. But almost all mammals are born alive. A baby whale is born out of its mother's body. It is called a calf.

A humpback whale calf grows in its mother's body for almost a year. All summer this mother whale swam in the cold waters of the northern Pacific Ocean while her baby grew inside her body.

At the end of the summer the cold water began to freeze. So the whales swam south to the warmer ocean. The warm water is a perfect place for a newborn baby whale.

Whales are gigantic at birth. This calf was fourteen feet long when it was born—about the size of a canoe.

The mother pushed her new baby gently to the water's surface. It quickly filled its lungs with air. Its mother needs fresh air too.

Humpback whales have two breathing holes at the top of their heads. They are called blowholes. The whales breathe through these holes the way we breathe through our noses.

When a whale comes up for air, it blows out the old air from its lungs. The air comes out of the blowholes on the top of its head. This air is mixed with tiny drops of water. When people see the spray shooting up, they say that the whale is spouting. Some spouts shoot as high as twenty-five feet into the air.

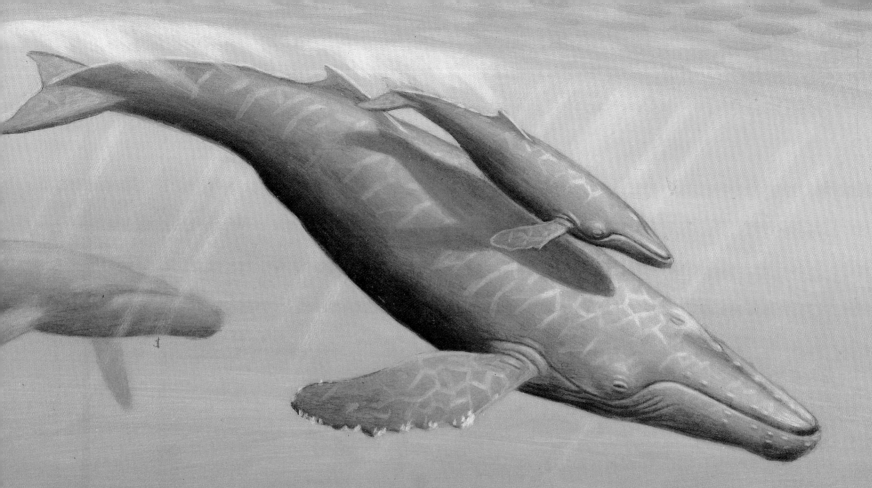

After the whale spouts, it breathes fresh air into its lungs. Some whales can swim for more than an hour without needing more air!

Now the baby humpback has plenty of air in its lungs. The mother and her calf dive down again.

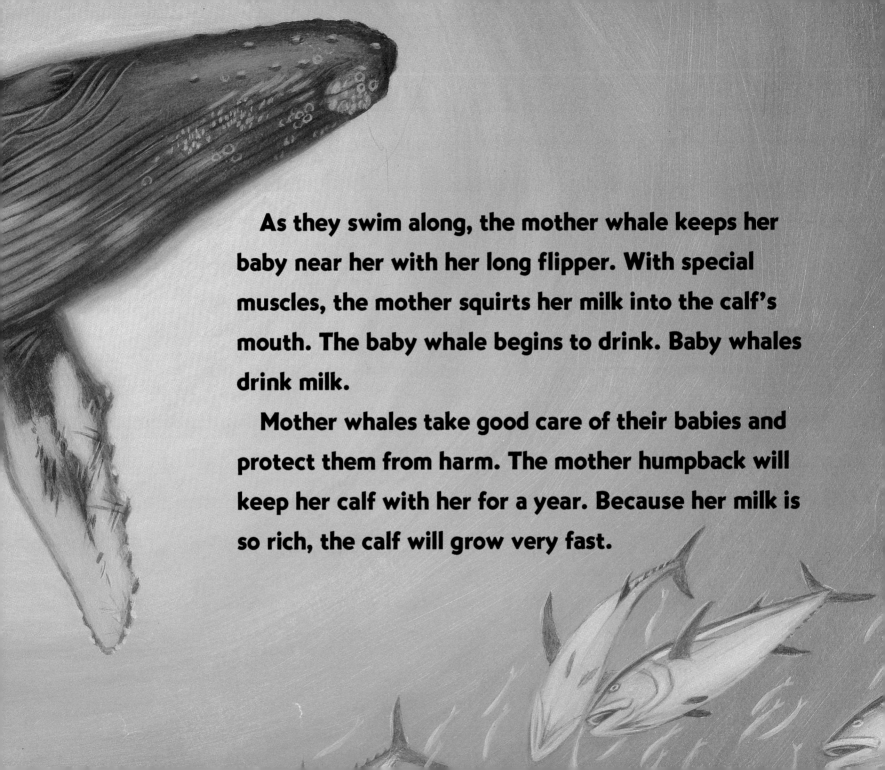

As they swim along, the mother whale keeps her baby near her with her long flipper. With special muscles, the mother squirts her milk into the calf's mouth. The baby whale begins to drink. Baby whales drink milk.

Mother whales take good care of their babies and protect them from harm. The mother humpback will keep her calf with her for a year. Because her milk is so rich, the calf will grow very fast.

All mammals are warm-blooded. Whales are warm-blooded too. The temperature inside a whale's body is always the same. Even in the coldest water. Even in warm water.

Fish are different. Fish are cold-blooded. Their body temperature changes if the water temperature changes.

People are warm-blooded mammals too. You may feel chilly, or you may feel very warm. But when you take your temperature with a thermometer, it will always be the same—about 98.6 degrees Fahrenheit.

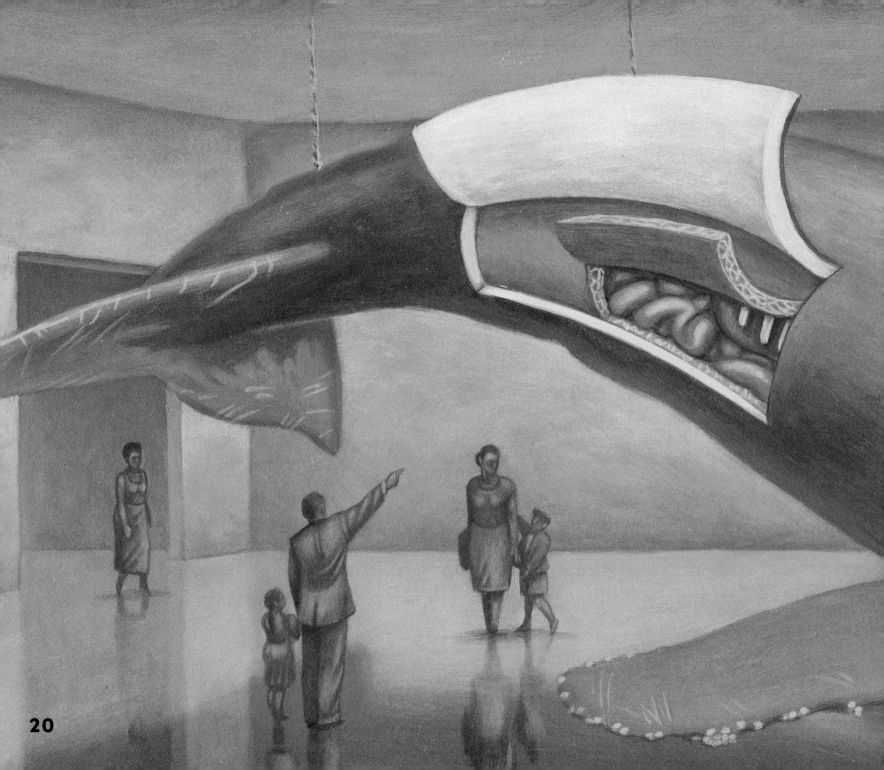

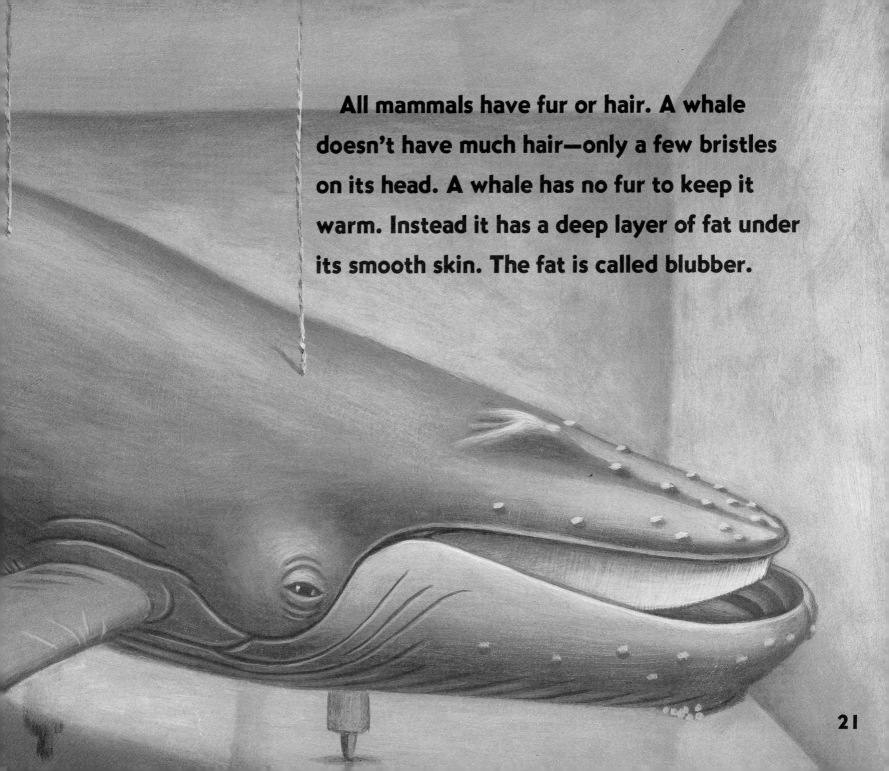

All mammals have fur or hair. A whale doesn't have much hair—only a few bristles on its head. A whale has no fur to keep it warm. Instead it has a deep layer of fat under its smooth skin. The fat is called blubber.

Whales can make many different sounds. The sounds are like songs. They can echo like distant thunder. They can creak like a swinging door. Sometimes the notes say "wheep-wheep-wheep." People do not know what the sounds mean, but they love to listen to whale songs.

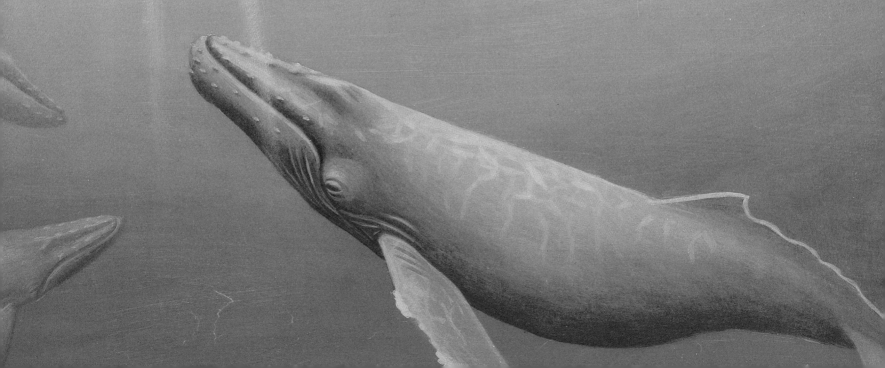

In late spring the humpback whales will leave the warm ocean. They travel back to their chilly summer homes.

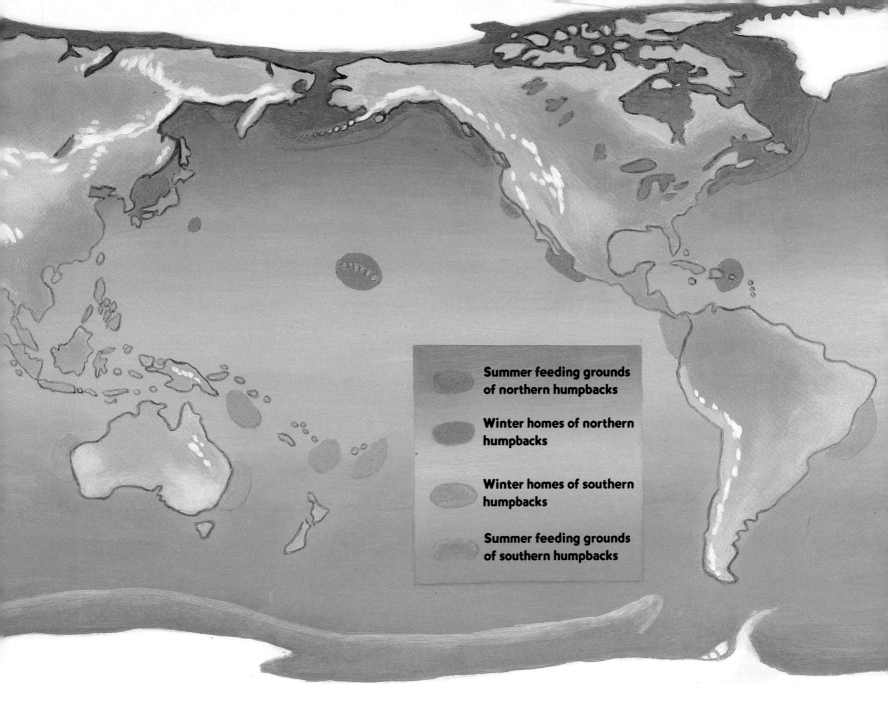

Summer feeding grounds
of northern humpbacks

Winter homes of northern
humpbacks

Winter homes of southern
humpbacks

Summer feeding grounds
of southern humpbacks

The water there is full of krill, the tiny animals that whales love to eat.

Humpbacks are baleen whales. Baleen whales have no teeth. Instead of teeth, hundreds of thin feathery plates, called baleen, hang from the whale's upper jaw. The baleen acts like a strainer that catches krill in the whale's mouth.

The mother humpback whale and her calf begin their long, slow journey to the north.

Soon the little whale will begin to eat the same food as its mother. But until it is old enough, it will drink its mother's milk.

Whales are mammals. Baby whales drink milk. Just like you!

More Whale Facts

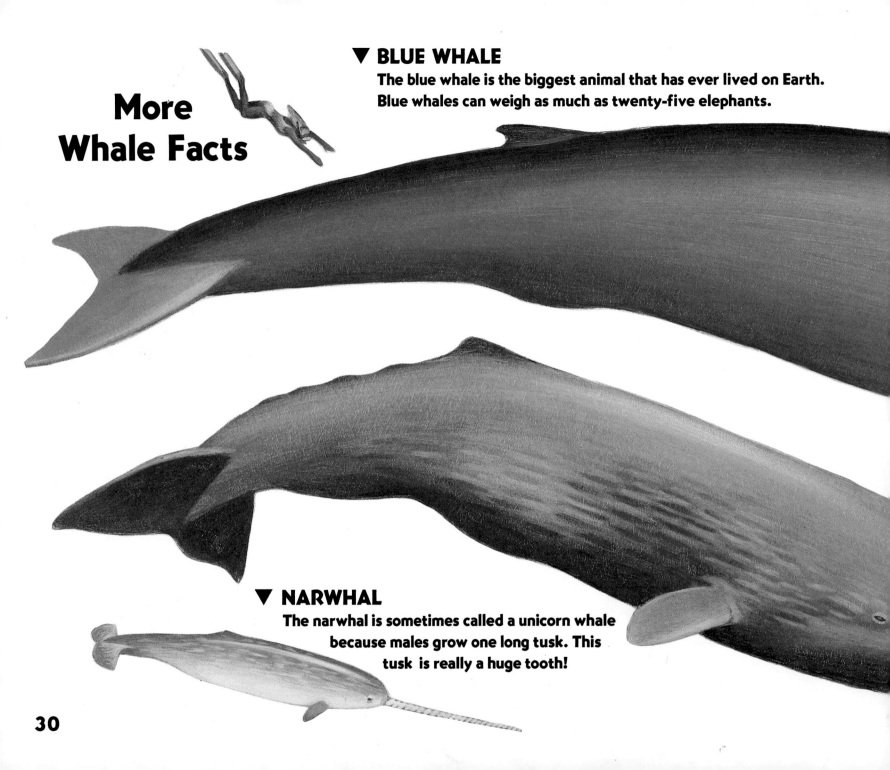

▼ BLUE WHALE

The blue whale is the biggest animal that has ever lived on Earth. Blue whales can weigh as much as twenty-five elephants.

▼ NARWHAL

The narwhal is sometimes called a unicorn whale because males grow one long tusk. This tusk is really a huge tooth!

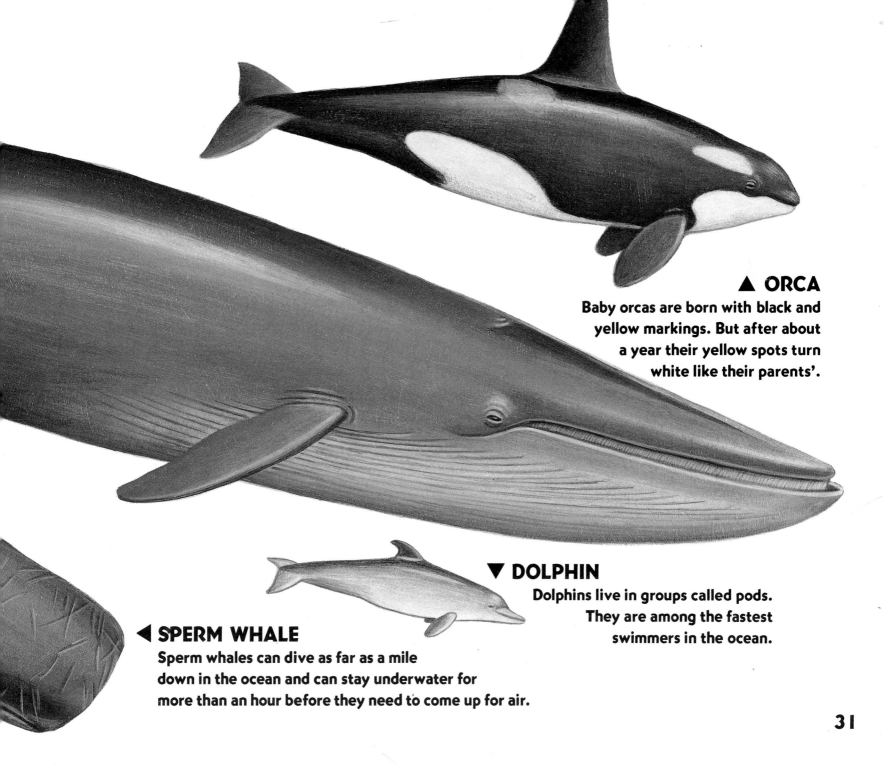

▲ ORCA

Baby orcas are born with black and yellow markings. But after about a year their yellow spots turn white like their parents'.

▼ DOLPHIN

Dolphins live in groups called pods. They are among the fastest swimmers in the ocean.

◀ SPERM WHALE

Sperm whales can dive as far as a mile down in the ocean and can stay underwater for more than an hour before they need to come up for air.

Where Can I See a Whale?

The best places to see a whale are New England in the summertime and Hawaii or California in the winter. If you are in any of these areas, you can call the following places for information about whale-watching tours:

THE NEW ENGLAND AQUARIUM
Central Wharf
Boston, MA 02110
(617) 973–5200

THE MONTEREY CHAMBER OF COMMERCE
Monterey, CA 93940
(408) 649–1770

THE HAWAII CHAMBER OF COMMERCE
180 Kinoole Street, Suite 118
Hilo, HI 96720
(808) 935–7178